learn to draw
Safari Animals

Step-by-step instructions for more than 25 exotic animals

ILLUSTRATED BY ROBBIN CUDDY

This library edition published in 2016 by Walter Foster Jr.,
an imprint of Quarto Publishing Group USA Inc.
6 Orchard Road, Suite 100
Lake Forest, CA 92630

Distributed in the United States and Canada by
Lerner Publisher Services
241 First Avenue North
Minneapolis, MN 55401 U.S.A.
www.lernerbooks.com

First Library Edition

Library of Congress Cataloging-in-Publication Data

Learn to draw safari animals : step-by-step instructions for more than 25 exotic animals /
Illustrated by Robbin Cuddy. -- First Library Edition.
    pages cm
  ISBN 978-1-939581-67-9
1. Animals in art--Juvenile literature. 2. Wildlife art--Juvenile literature. 3. Drawing--Technique--
Juvenile literature. I. Cuddy, Robbin, illustrator.
  NC780.L34 2016
  743.6--dc23

                                                                            2015007020

012016
1765

9 8 7 6 5 4 3 2 1

Table of Contents

Tools & Materials 4

How to Use This Book 5

Safari Map 6

African Elephant 8

Gazelle 10

Giraffe 12

Hippopotamus 14

Hyena.. 16

Lemur 18

Impala 20

Kangaroo 22

Leopard 24

Meerkat 26

Lion 28

Mountain Gorilla 30

Nile Crocodile 32

Okapi 34

Oryx 36

Kudu.. 38

Cheetah... 40

Grey Crowned Crane 42

Bat-Eared Fox.. 44

Baboon 46

Aardvark 48

Zebra 50

Wildebeest 52

Yellow Mongoose 54

Warthog 56

Rock Hyrax 58

Rhinoceros... 60

Ostrich... 62

Mini Quiz Answers 64

Tools & Materials

There's more than one way to bring safari animals to life on paper—
you can use crayons, markers, colored pencils, or even paints.
Just be sure you have plenty of good animal colors—yellows,
reds, grays, and browns.

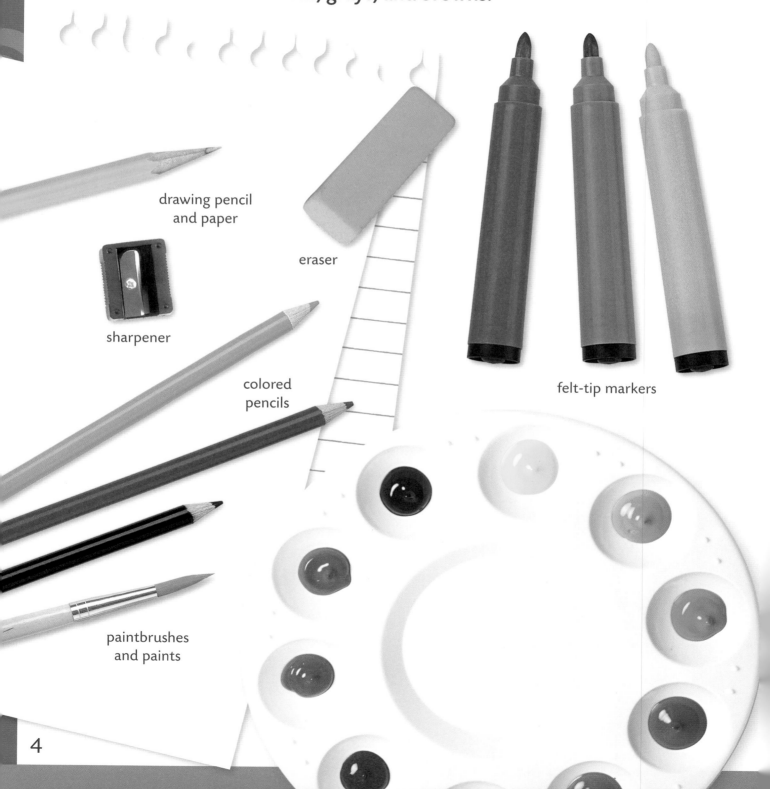

drawing pencil
and paper

eraser

sharpener

colored
pencils

felt-tip markers

paintbrushes
and paints

How to Use This Book

The drawings in this book are made up of basic shapes, such as circles, triangles, and rectangles. Practice drawing the shapes below.

Draw a square

Draw a circle

Draw an oval

Draw a rectangle

Draw a triangle

Notice how these drawings begin with basic shapes.

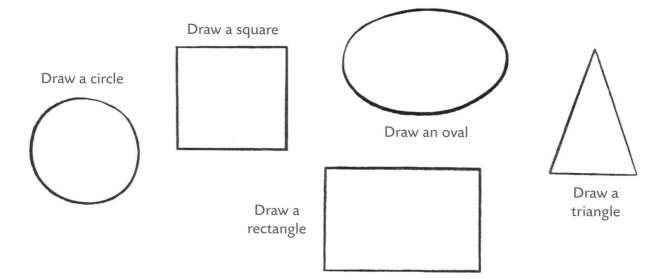

In this book, you'll learn about the size, weight, location, diet, and appearance of each featured safari animal. Look for mini quizzes along the way to learn new and interesting facts!

Look for this symbol, and check your answers on page 64!

Safari Map

Get ready to embark on an artistic journey through the world's most exciting wildernesses—from the Australian Outback to the African Serengeti! Look at the map below to see where you'll be traveling.

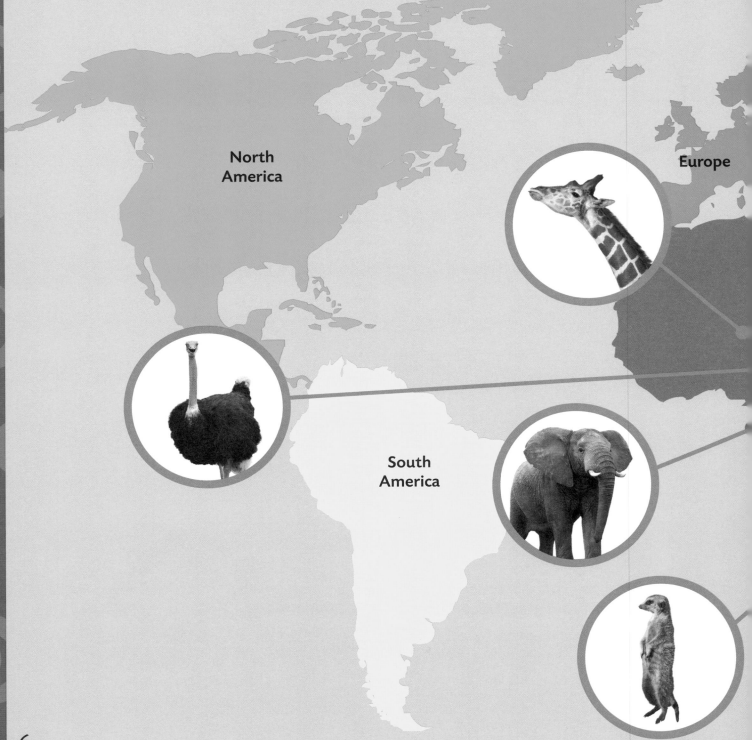

North
America

Europe

South
America

Asia

Africa

Australia

7

African Elephant

Location:
African savannas,
grasslands, and
forests

Size: 14 feet
tall at the
shoulder
Weight:
8 tons

Did You Know?

An African elephant's
trunk has two "fingers"
at the tip for grabbing
and foraging. The trunk
is also used for drinking,
breathing, and even hugging
other elephants.

Diet: Grasses,
bushes, fruit, and
other plants

8

African elephants are the largest land mammals alive today. These intelligent creatures have wide ears, long trunks, ivory tusks, and thick, wrinkly skin.

Fun Fact!

Just like dolphins, humans, and the great apes, elephants have the ability to recognize themselves in mirrors!

Gazelle

Size: 43 inches tall at the shoulder
Weight: 165 pounds

Location: Asia and Africa

Diet: Grasses, shoots, and leaves

Did You Know?

Gazelles don't have to drink water! Their bodies can extract enough water from the plants in their diet.

Gazelles are known for their unique bounding run. These fast, graceful animals have hoofed feet, ringed horns, and bodies similar to deer.

1

2

3

4

5

6

Mini Quiz

True or false: Gazelles are solitary animals and prefer to travel alone.

(Answer on page 64)

11

Giraffe

Size: Up to 19 feet tall
Weight: Between 2,600 pounds (females) and 4,250 pounds (males)

Location: African grasslands and woodlands

Diet: Shoots and leaves

Male giraffes are called "bulls," female giraffes are called "cows," and baby giraffes are called "calves."

Did You Know?

The giraffe has a very long neck, tall legs, a pair of horns, and a wiry tail. The tallest land animal on earth, a male giraffe can reach 19 feet tall!

Giraffes are surprisingly fast; they can run more than 30 miles per hour!

Fun Fact!

13

Hippopotamus

Did You Know?

To keep cool, hippos spend most of their days in rivers and lakes with their nostrils, eyes, and ears poking above the water.

These large creatures have little round ears, bulging eyes, and thick gray skin. They can open their mouths very wide to show off their giant teeth.

Fun Fact!

Hippopotamus means "river horse" in Greek. These graceful swimmers can actually walk on the bottoms of lakes and rivers.

15

Hyena

Size: 3 feet tall at the shoulder
Weight: 180 pounds

Diet: Meat and bones

Location: Asia and Africa

Did You Know?

Hyenas make strange whoops, yells, and chirps that sound like human laughter.

The hyena is a mischievous carnivore that resembles a wild dog. A skilled hunter and scavenger, this animal has a powerful jaw, neck, and shoulders for tearing apart prey.

Mini Quiz

What is the term for a group of hyenas that live together?
A. Pack
B. Pod
C. Herd
D. Cackle
(Answer on page 64)

17

Lemur

Size: 3.5 to 28 inches long, not including the tail
Weight: Up to 15 pounds
Diet: Leaves, fruits, insects, and birds' eggs
Location: Madagascar and the Comoros Islands

Did You Know?

A lemur's eyes work well in low light, giving them great night vision.

Lemurs are monkey-like primates that have round eyes, small muzzles, and five fingers on each hand and foot. They spend most of their time among the trees.

Mini Quiz

Which of the following is the smallest species of lemur?
A. Ring-tailed lemur
B. Madame Berthe's mouse lemur
C. Black lemur
D. Brown mouse lemur
(Answer on page 64)

Impala

Diet:
Grasses, leaves,
and soft shoots

Size: 3 feet
tall at the
shoulder
Weight: 135
pounds

Location:
Eastern and
southern Africa

Did You Know?

Impalas live near
water along the edges
of woodlands and
grasslands.

An impala is a slender antelope with a long neck, a pair of wavy horns, and a two-toned coat with white markings.

21

Kangaroo

Size: 7 feet
Weight: 120 pounds

Diet:
Grasses, leaves, and fruit

Did You Know?

A baby kangaroo (called a "joey") climbs into its mother's pouch right after birth, where it can feed and continue developing for the next 10 months.

Location:
Australia

The kangaroo has large ears, a small mouth, and powerful hind legs. Its long, tapering tail helps the kangaroo balance while standing still.

1

2

3

4

5

6

Mini Quiz

How high can a kangaroo jump?
A. 2 feet
B. 3 feet
C. 6 feet
D. 10 feet
(Answer on page 64)

23

Leopard

Size: Nearly 30 inches tall at the shoulder
Weight: 200 pounds

Diet: Meat from deer, antelope, and other prey

Location: Africa and Asia

Did You Know?

Leopards often bring their food up into the trees to protect it from other animals.

Known for its beautifully spotted coat, this striking feline is skilled at hunting, running, swimming, and climbing trees.

Fun Fact! How can you tell a leopard from a jaguar? Look at the coat! A jaguar's markings (called "rosettes") contain black spots.

Meerkat

Size: Nearly 1 foot (length of head and body)
Weight: 2 pounds

Diet: Fruit, insects, lizards, and birds

Location: Southwestern Africa

Did You Know?

Meerkats live in complex burrows made up of underground tunnels and chambers. These homes stay cool even on the hottest days.

Meerkats are adorable critters with pointed muzzles and black eye patches. They are social animals that live in packs of about 5 to 25 individuals.

1

2

3

Fun Fact!

Meerkats are often photographed in an upright position, which helps them spot predators. Upon detecting a threat, a meerkat warns the rest of its pack with a high-pitched call.

4

5

6

Lion

Details

Size: Up to 40 inches tall
Weight: Up to 500 pounds
Diet: Antelopes, zebras, wildebeests, monkeys, hippos, and more
Location: African grasslands and savannas, India's Gir Forest

Did You Know?

Adult male and female lions look quite a bit different from each other. A male lion has a large mane around its head and neck and is much larger, sometimes weighing hundreds of pounds more than a female.

Dubbed "King of Beasts," the lion is a large, regal feline that lives in a *pride* (or group). Lions use their deep, distinct roar to define their pride's territory.

Fun Fact!

Born blind, lions do not open their eyes until one to two weeks after birth. They are also born with spots on their coats, which fade as the lions mature.

Mountain Gorilla

Size: Up to 6 feet tall (while standing)
Weight: Up to 485 pounds

Diet: Leaves, shoots, roots, and fruit

Fun Fact!

Mountain gorillas are extremely intelligent animals and can learn sign language!

Location: African tropical forests

30

Mountain gorillas are among the world's largest primates. They have hairless faces, large nostrils, and a distinct brow ridge.

Mini Quiz

True or false: Mountain gorillas generally walk upright on their hind legs like humans.

(Answer on page 64)

31

Nile Crocodile

Details

Size: Up to 20 feet long
Weight: 500 to 2,000 pounds
Diet: Fish, birds, and a variety of other animals
Location: Madagascar, the Nile Basin, and sub-Saharan Africa

Did You Know?

Crocodiles spend most of their time in water, such as rivers, estuaries, and marshlands. As they swim, they keep most of their body hidden while their nostrils, ears, and eyes poke above the surface.

One of the largest reptiles on earth, the Nile crocodile is a stealthy predator with thick, plated skin and a long snout full of sharp teeth.

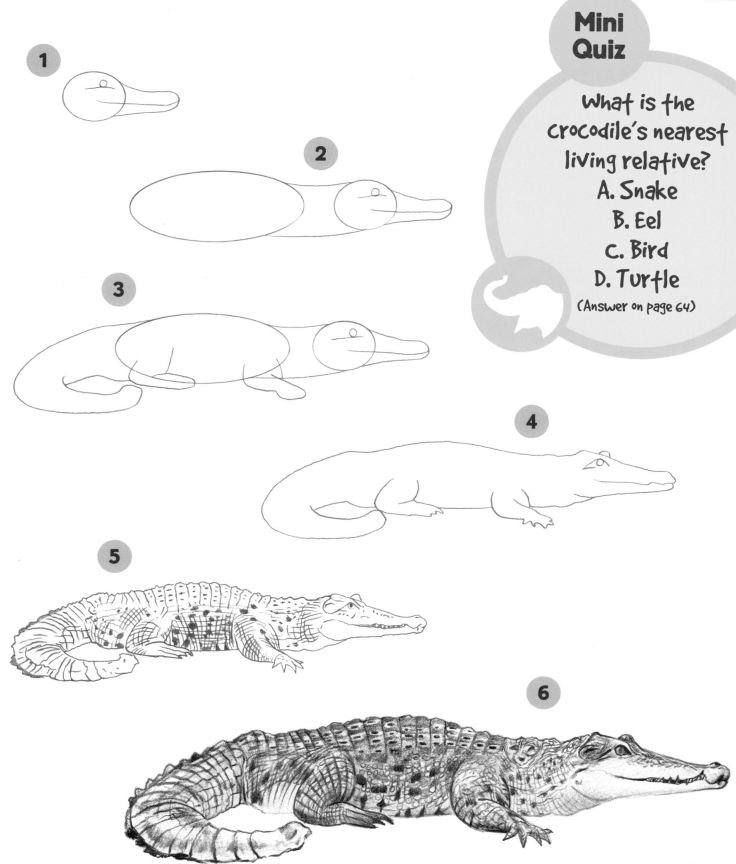

1

2

3

4

5

6

Mini Quiz

What is the crocodile's nearest living relative?
A. Snake
B. Eel
C. Bird
D. Turtle
(Answer on page 64)

33

Okapi

Details

Size: 5 feet tall at the shoulder
Weight: 100 pounds (female) to 600 pounds (male)
Diet: Grasses, leaves, and fruits
Location: African rainforests

Did You Know?

The okapi might look part zebra, but it is a relative of the giraffe. The okapi and the giraffe both have long grasping tongues.

This hoofed animal is known for its very distinct coloring. It has a reddish-brown body, black-and-white striped legs, and white facial markings.

Fun Fact! The okapi is known to eat both charcoal and red clay! Some scientists think this provides necessary salts and minerals. Others think the charcoal and clay counteract plant toxins in the okapi's diet.

Oryx

Diet:
Grasses and roots

Size: 40 to 54 inches tall
Weight: 160 to 525 pounds

Location: Desert and plains of Africa and the Middle East

Did You Know?

The oryx is well adapted to the desert heat. This animal has a special nose with lots of capillaries that cool its blood as it breathes.

The oryx is an antelope with a full chest, long legs, and two thin, lengthy horns. Their coats range in color from white and gray to brown and red.

Fun Fact! When viewed from the side, an oryx appears to have just one horn, which led to its nickname, "the Arabian Unicorn."

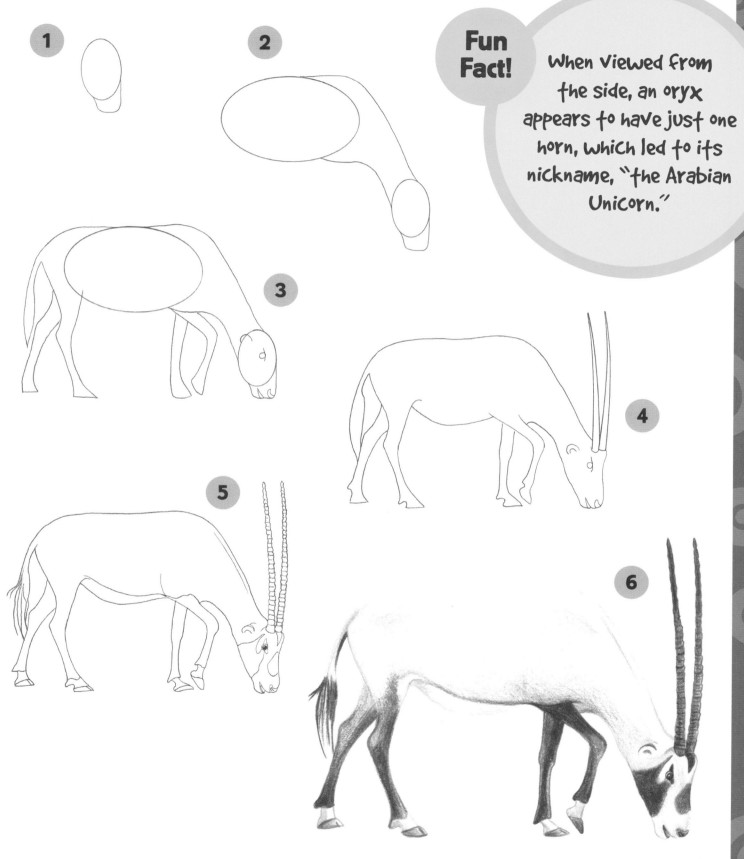

37

Kudu

Diet:
Grasses and roots

Location:
Desert and plains of Africa and the Middle East

Size: 60 inches tall (greater kudu) and 40 inches tall (lesser kudu)
Weight: Up to 600 pounds

The two species of kudu are the greater kudu and the lesser kudu. The greater kudu is larger in size and is one of the tallest antelopes on earth, second only to the eland.

Did You Know?

This antelope has thin, white stripes over its torso and a short spinal crest that gives its back a humped appearance. Males also have beards and unique corkscrew horns.

Fun Fact! A mature male's corkscrew horns often measure more than 2 feet long and make about two and a half turns. Greater kudu males have the longest horns of any antelope in the world!

1

2

3

4

5

6

Cheetah

Details

Size: Up to 3 feet tall
Weight: 75 to 140 pounds
Diet: Birds, rabbits, and antelopes
Location: Grasslands of Africa

Fun Fact!

The cheetah is earth's fastest land animal, reaching speeds of more than 70 miles per hour!

This furry feline has a black-spotted yellow coat with a white underbelly. Its long legs, spine, and powerful paws make it an incredibly fast predator.

Mini Quiz

True or false: Cheetahs can go more than four days without a drink of water.

(Answer on page 64)

41

Grey Crowned Crane

Location:
South and East
Africa

Diet:
Grasses, grains,
seeds, insects,
worms, fish, and
other small animals

Size: 3.5 feet
tall
Weight: 8
pounds

Did You Know?

The grey crowned crane
is a non-migratory bird
that makes its home in
the savannas, wetlands,
and flatlands of South
and East Africa.

This elegant bird has long legs, a gray body, white wings, white cheeks with red markings, and a golden crown of feathers.

1

2

3

4

5

6

43

Bat-Eared Fox

Did You Know?

The bat-eared fox's large ears aren't just for hearing! They contain lots of blood vessels that give off body heat and help the fox stay cool under the African sun.

The bat-eared fox has large, wide ears and a small, pointed face. This canine has a yellow and gray grizzled coat with darker fur on its face, legs, and tail.

Fun Fact!

The bat-eared fox loves to eat termites. one fox can eat more than a million termites per year!

Baboon

Diet:
Grasses, fruits, seeds, bark, birds, rodents, and other animals

Size: Up to 45 inches long
Weight:
30 pounds (female) to 60 pounds (male)

Location:
Arid regions of Africa and the Middle East

Did You Know?

The male baboon has a pair of sharp canines, which it bares when fighting other male baboons.

46

The baboon is an aggressive monkey with a long snout and a long, arched tail. These social animals communicate through vocalizations, gestures, and expressions.

1

2

3

4

5

6

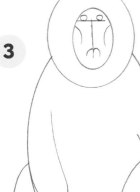

Aardvark

Fun Fact!

The aardvark's worm-like tongue can be more than a foot long! The tongue is sticky to help catch ants, termites, and other critters in the dirt.

48

The aardvark has small eyes, large ears, a thick tail, and spade-like claws. It uses its long, sensitive snout to find food in the ground.

Mini Quiz

What does the word "aardvark" mean in the Afrikaans language?
A. Short kangaroo
B. Insect eater
C. Tongue digger
D. Earth pig
(Answer on page 64)

49

Zebra

Size: Up to 5 feet tall at the shoulder
Weight: 450 to 1,000 pounds

Diet: Grasses

Location: African grasslands

Did You Know?

Zebras can sleep standing up! To protect themselves, zebras sleep only when huddled together in a large group.

The zebra is a horse-like mammal with a distinct black-and-white striped coat. It has a thick, strong neck topped with a short mane.

Mini Quiz

What color is a zebra's skin?
A. Black
B. Pink
C. White
D. Tan
(Answer on page 64)

Wildebeest

Did You Know?

Wildebeests live in large herds to protect themselves from their many African predators, including cheetahs, leopards, lions, hyenas, and even crocodiles.

Also called a "gnu," the wildebeest is a large, ox-like antelope. It has a long tail, beard, and mane and a set of thick, sharp horns that curl forward.

Fun Fact!

The wildebeest migration in late May is a spectacular event. More than 1.5 million wildebeests travel north through the Serengeti in search of water and food.

Yellow Mongoose

Details

Size: Up to 38 inches long
Weight: 1 pound
Diet: Insects, rodents, small mammals, birds, snakes, and eggs
Location: Southern Africa

Did You Know?

These brave little carnivores have quick reflexes. Even fast-striking snakes can fall victim to the mongoose!

The yellow mongoose is a small mammal with a long body and white-tipped tail. Their grizzled coats range from gray to yellow and orange.

Fun Fact!

Yellow mongooses live in colonies that inhabit underground burrow systems. Sometimes they share burrows and tunnels with squirrels and meerkats.

55

Warthog

Size: 30 inches tall at the shoulder
Weight: Up to 250 pounds

Diet: Grasses, roots, and bulbs

Location: Africa

Did You Know?

The warthog uses its snout and strong feet to dig for bulbs and roots to eat.

A relative of the pig, the beastly warthog has hoofed feet, a very large head and snout, and two pairs of tusks that curve upward.

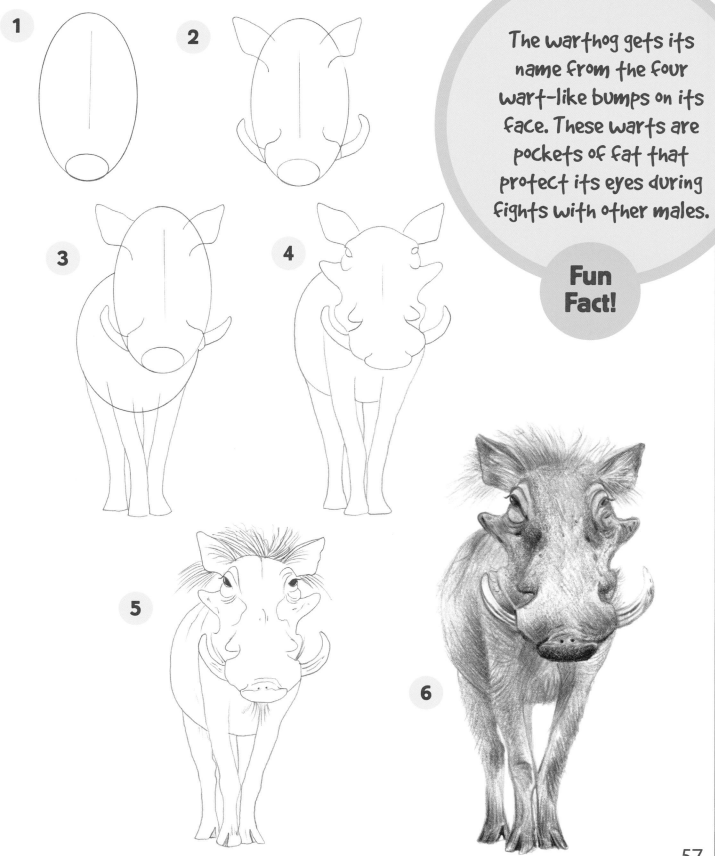

The warthog gets its name from the four wart-like bumps on its face. These warts are pockets of fat that protect its eyes during fights with other males.

Fun Fact!

Rock Hyrax

Details

Size: Up to 20 inches long
Weight: 10 pounds
Diet: Grasses, shrubs, roots, fruits, and insects
Location: Africa and areas of the Middle East

Did You Know?

The rock hyrax is active during the day and lives in groups of up to 80 individuals, who work together to find food.

The rock hyrax is a small mammal that lives in rock fissures. With a round body and small nose, eyes, and ears, this cute creature is rodent-like in appearance.

Fun Fact!

Scientists believe ancient ancestors of the rock hyrax might have been as large as modern horses! The hyrax is also a distant relative of other giant mammals, such as manatees and elephants.

Rhinoceros

Size: 7 feet tall at the shoulder
Weight: Up to 5 tons

Diet: Grasses, leaves, trees, and shrubs

Fun Fact!

The word rhinoceros comes from the Greek words rhino (meaning "nose") and keras (meaning "horn").

Location: Africa and Asia

The rhinoceros is a huge, thick-skinned mammal with three toes on each foot. African rhinoceroses have two fibrous horns, which can grow up to 5 feet long.

1

2

3

4

5

6

Mini Quiz

What distinguishes the black rhinoceros from the white rhinoceros?
A. The color of the skin
B. The shape of the lip
C. The size of the ears
D. All of the above
(Answer on page 64)

Ostrich

Details

Size: 9 feet tall
Weight: 300 pounds
Diet: Leaves, grasses, seeds, and insects
Location: African savannas and deserts

Fun Fact!

Ostrich eggs are the largest bird eggs in the world. They typically weigh up to 5 pounds and have a circumference of about 18 inches.

The ostrich is both the largest living bird and the fastest! It has a black or brown body, a long neck, and tall, strong legs.

Mini Quiz

True or false: Despite its wings, the ostrich cannot fly.

(Answer on page 64)

Mini Quiz Answers

Page 11: False. Gazelles travel in herds to defend themselves against predators.

Page 17: D. A group of hyenas is called a "cackle."

Page 19: B. The Madame Berthe's mouse lemur, the smallest lemur in the world, weighs about an ounce.

Page 23: C. A kangaroo can jump 6 feet high.

Page 31: False. Mountain gorillas primarily use knuckle walking to get around, which involves all four limbs.

Page 33: C. Although crocodiles may look like giant lizards, their nearest living relative is the bird.

Page 41: True. Cheetahs have adapted well to an environment with limited water and can go up to ten days without a drink.

Page 49: D. Aardvark means "earth pig" in the Afrikaans language.

Page 51: A. Beneath the zebra's black-and-white coat is black skin.

Page 61: B. A black rhino has a hooked mouth for eating trees, while a white rhino has a flat or squared lip for eating grass.

Page 63: True. Ostriches may be fast runners, but they cannot fly.